THIS BOOK
BELONGS TO

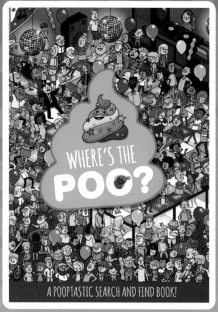
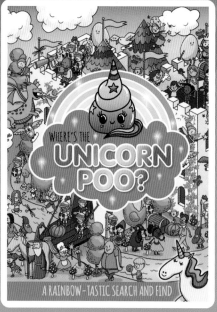
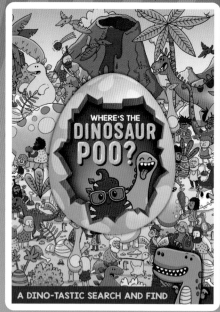
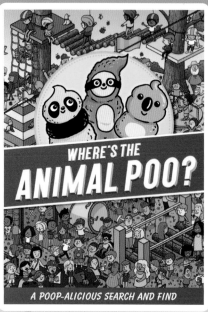
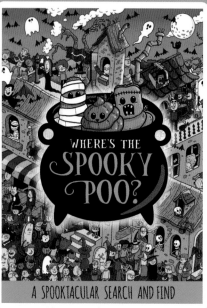

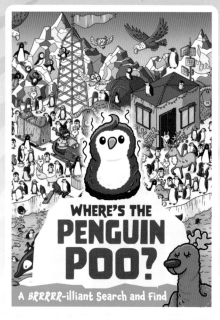

ORCHARD

MEET THE POOS

Ho, oh no! It's time to deliver this year's Christmas presents but the festive poos have got lost! Can you find them in the following scenes and help save Christmas?

RUBY

The reindeer poo lights up the way for Santa's sleigh with her red nose, but she's still hard to spot!

FROSTY

The frozen poo is the cool kid of the group – he always knows how to break the ice! Just don't get on his wrong side, or he might have a meltdown ...

CANDY

The peppermint poo loves celebrating Christmas. She's the opposite of a party pooper!

AIRPORT DROP-OFF

Candy is flying home to visit her family for the holidays. Can you see her and the other festive poos at the airport?

CRAZY GOLF

When he needs to unwind, Santa loves to play golf. Can you find him and his friends hiding on the course?

STOCKING FILLERS

The poos have got lost in the North Pole while helping to pack Santa's stockings. Can you find them?

ODD ONE OUT!
One of these stockings is not like the others – can you spot it?

CHRISTMAS WISHLIST

Jolly's left her Christmas shopping to the last minute! Can you see her looking for presents in this toy shop?

FESTIVE FEAST

Clean-up on aisle five! Can you spot Ruby shopping for her Christmas dinner before the supermarket cleaners do?

ONE OF A KIND

Brrrr! Frosty and his poo friends are caught in the middle of a blizzard! Can you spot them in the snow?

ODD ONE OUT!
One of these snowflakes is different to the others. Can you find it?

SWEET TREATS

Candy is skipping the advent calendar this Christmas and going straight to the sweet factory! Can you spot her?

CHRISTMAS DOWN UNDER

G'day mate! The poos have come to Australia for Christmas in the sun! Can you spot them hiding on the beach?

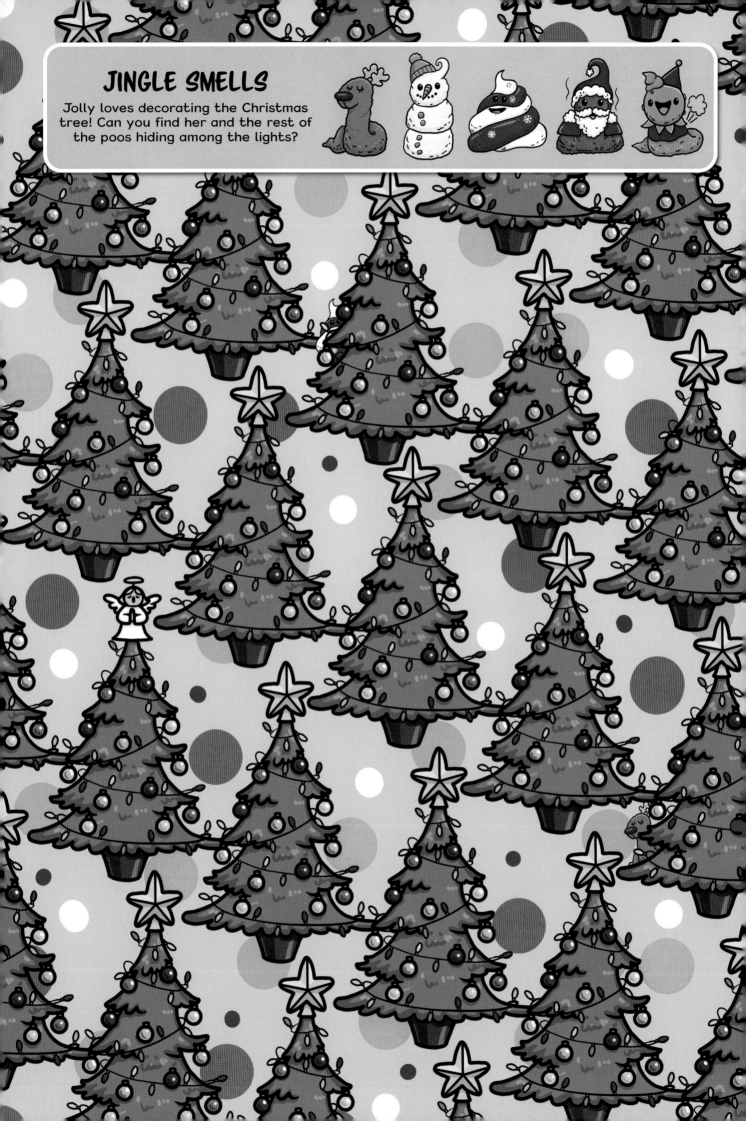

JINGLE SMELLS

Jolly loves decorating the Christmas tree! Can you find her and the rest of the poos hiding among the lights?

ODD ONE OUT!
One of the Christmas trees is not like the others. Can you see it?

ICE, ICE, BABY

The festive poos have arrived in a winter wonderland to go ice skating! Can you find Frosty and his friends?

JOYEUX NOËL

Oui, oui! The poos have arrived in Paris just in time for the holidays! But where are they hiding?

GIFTS GALORE

It's time to open presents! Will the poos get everything on their wishlists? Find them hiding among the gifts.

ODD ONE OUT!
One of these gifts is different to the others. Can you spot it?

NUTCRACKER BALLET

The poos are on their way to see a very special Christmas show! Can you spot them dancing in the crowd?

OH CHRISTMAS TREE!

Santa's favourite part of Christmas is picking out the perfect tree. Can you find him and his friends in the forest?

ANSWERS

Now try and find the extra items hidden in each scene.

AIRPORT DROP-OFF

A baguette ☐

Two light bulbs ☐

Seven children's suitcases ☐

Four white tags ☐

Two green dinosaurs ☐

Twenty-two backpacks ☐

Three planes ☐

Two footprints ☐

Five coffee cups ☐

A pair of purple headphones ☐

CRAZY GOLF

Six flags ☐

A windmill ☐

Three cats ☐

A spider ☐

Three frogs ☐

A banana ☐

Three butterflies ☐

A bird eating chips ☐

Bird poo ☐

Three water bottles ☐

STOCKING FILLERS

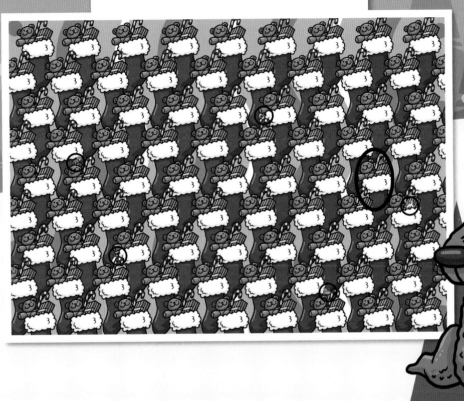

CHRISTMAS WISHLIST

Nine walkie-talkies ☐

Nine roller-skates ☐

Five pink unicorns ☐

Six penguins ☐

Nine mermaids ☐

Seven skittles ☐

Eight American footballs ☐

Four kites ☐

Two rocking horses ☐

Six shuttlecocks ☐

FESTIVE FEAST

Four pineapples ☐

A head of lettuce ☐

Four tigers ☐

One hockey stick ☐

Seven bananas ☐

Five boxes of tea ☐

Eight tomatoes ☐

Nine trolleys ☐

A pair of green trousers ☐

Nine packs of toilet roll ☐

ONE OF A KIND

SWEET TREATS

Two fried eggs ☐

A stool ☐

A candy cane tree ☐

A chicken ☐

Two top hats ☐

Four flowers ☐

Seven chocolate bars ☐

A dog ☐

Seventeen cardboard boxes ☐

Four purple scoops ☐

CHRISTMAS DOWN UNDER

Three umbrellas ☐

Eighteen fish ☐

Two boomerangs ☐

A green bird ☐

Two guitars ☐

An ice cream with three scoops ☐

Three fishing rods ☐

Nine grey pigeons ☐

A puppet ☐

Three surfboards ☐

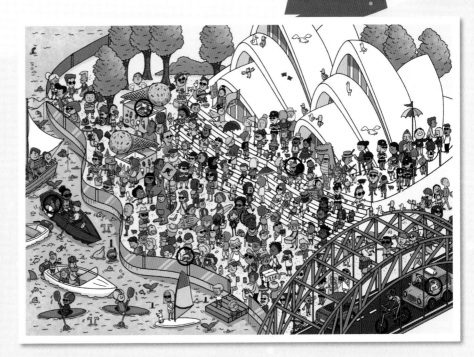

JINGLE SMELLS

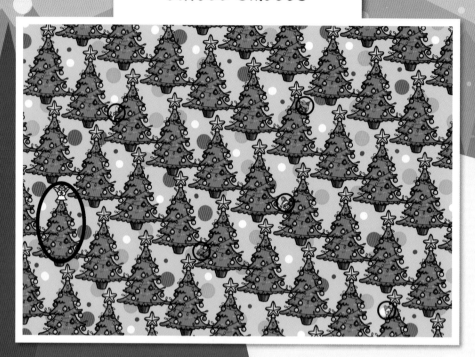

ICE, ICE, BABY

Three ice hockey players ☐

Five penguins ☐

Three white beards ☐

A pair of red shoes ☐

Two tutus ☐

Six red scarves ☐

A spilt drink ☐

Six mountains ☐

Three birds ☐

A duck ☐

JOYEUX NOËL

- Two black teapots
- Four mopeds
- A daisy chain
- Two poodles
- A flower pot
- Two people doing handstands
- A Mona Lisa
- Three croissants
- A dropped ice cream
- A wheel of cheese

GIFTS GALORE

Did you find me? If you're stuck, try visiting Ice, Ice, Baby again.

NUTCRACKER BALLET

Four maps ☐

A dragonfly ☐

Three arrows pointing upwards ☐

An accordion ☐

Two identical twins ☐

A banjo ☐

Two people giving piggybacks ☐

A burger ☐

A couple shaking hands ☐

A bear ☐

OH CHRISTMAS TREE!

Nine wreaths ☐

Three hedgehogs ☐

A bird eating a cookie ☐

Two rabbits ☐

A walking stick ☐

Two squirrels ☐

Three gingerbread men ☐

A Santa lookalike ☐

Nine miniature trees ☐

Three dogs ☐

ORCHARD BOOKS
First published in Great Britain in 2022 by Hodder & Stoughton © 2022 Hodder & Stoughton
Illustrations by Dynamo Limited   Additional images © Shutterstock
A CIP catalogue record for this book is available from the British Library
ISBN 978 1 40836 864 0   Printed and bound in China   3 5 7 9 10 8 6 4 2

Orchard Books, an imprint of Hachette Children's Group
Part of Hodder & Stoughton, Carmelite House, 50 Victoria Embankment, London, EC4Y 0DZ
An Hachette UK Company   www.hachette.co.uk   www.hachettechildrens.co.uk

FSC
MIX
Paper from
responsible sources
FSC® C188448